D0394621

ALFRED A. KNOPF

1915 · 100 YEARS · 2015

ALSO BY OLIVER SACKS

Migraine

Awakenings

A Leg to Stand On

The Man Who Mistook His Wife for a Hat

Seeing Voices

An Anthropologist on Mars

The Island of the Colorblind

Uncle Tungsten

Oaxaca Journal

Musicophilia

The Mind's Eye

Hallucinations

On the Move

Gratitude

Oliver Sacks

Gratitude

ALFRED A. KNOPF NEW YORK TORONTO 2015

This Is a Borzoi Book
Published by Alfred A. Knopf and Alfred A. Knopf Canada

Copyright © 2015 by the Estate of Oliver Sacks
Foreword copyright © 2015 Kate Edgar and Bill Hayes
Photographs copyright © 2015 by Bill Hayes

All rights reserved. Published in the United States by
Alfred A. Knopf, a division of Random House LLC,
New York, and in Canada by Alfred A. Knopf of Canada,
a division of Penguin Random House
Canada Ltd., Toronto.

www.aaknopf.com
www.penguinrandomhouse.ca
www.oliversacks.com

Knopf, Borzoi Books, and the colophon are registered
trademarks of Penguin Random House LLC. Knopf Canada
and colophon are trademarks of Penguin
Random House Canada Ltd.

ISBN (USA) 978-0-451-49293-7 (hardcover);
978-0-451-49296-8 (eBook)
ISBN (Canada) 978-0-345-81136-3 (hardcover);
978-0-345-81137-0 (eBook)

Library of Congress Control Number: 2015952928

These pieces originally appeared in The New York Times
as follows: "Mercury" as "The Joy of Old Age" (July 6, 2013),
"My Own Life" (February 19, 2015), "My Periodic Table"
(July 24, 2015), and "Sabbath" (August 14, 2015).

Special thanks to Peter Catapano

Jacket design by Carol Devine Carson

Manufactured in the United States of America

First Edition

I am now face to face with dying,
but I am not finished with living.

Contents

Foreword

IN THIS QUARTET OF ESSAYS, written in the last two years of his life, Oliver Sacks faces aging, illness, and death with remarkable grace and clarity. The first essay, "Mercury," written in one sitting just days before his eightieth birthday in July 2013, celebrates the pleasures of old age—without dismissing the frailties of body and mind that may come with it.

Eighteen months later, shortly after completing a final draft of his memoir *On the Move*, Dr. Sacks learned that the rare form of melanoma in his eye, first diagnosed in 2005, had metastasized to his liver. There were very few treatment options for this particular type of cancer, and his physicians prognosticated that he might have as little as six months to live. Within days he had completed the essay "My Own Life," in which he expressed his overwhelming feeling of appreciation for a life well lived. And yet he hesitated to publish this immediately: Was it premature? Did he want to go public with the news of his terminal illness? A month later, literally as he entered surgery for a treatment that would give him several extra months of active life, he asked to have the essay sent to *The New York Times*, where it was published the next day. The enormous and sympathetic reaction to "My Own Life" was immensely gratifying to him.

In May, June, and early July of 2015, he enjoyed relative good health—writing, swimming, playing piano, and traveling. He wrote several essays during this period, including "My Periodic Table," in which he reflects on his lifelong love for the periodic table of the elements and on his own mortality.

By August, Dr. Sacks' health was declining rapidly, but he devoted his last energies to writing. The final piece in this book, "Sabbath," was particularly important to him, and he went over every word of the essay time and again, distilling it to its essence. It was published two weeks before his death on August 30, 2015.

—*Kate Edgar and Bill Hayes*

Gratitude

Mercury

L AST NIGHT I DREAMED about mercury—huge, shining globules of quicksilver rising and falling. Mercury is element number 80, and my dream is a reminder that on Tuesday, I will be eighty myself.

Elements and birthdays have been intertwined for me since boyhood, when I learned about atomic numbers. At eleven, I could say "I am sodium" (element 11), and now at seventy-nine, I am gold. A few years ago, when I gave a friend a bottle of mercury for his eightieth birthday—a special bottle that could neither leak nor break—he gave me a peculiar look, but later sent me a charming letter in which he joked, "I take a little every morning for my health."

Eighty! I can hardly believe it. I often feel that life is about to begin, only to realize it is almost over. My mother was the sixteenth of eighteen children; I was the youngest of her four sons, and almost the youngest of the vast cousinhood on her side of the family. I was always the youngest boy in my class at high school. I have retained this feeling of being the youngest, even though now I am almost the oldest person I know.

I thought I would die at forty-one, when I had a bad fall and broke a leg while mountaineering alone. I splinted the leg as best I could and started to lever myself down the mountain, clumsily, with my arms. In the long hours that followed, I was assailed by memories, both good and bad. Most were in a mode of gratitude—gratitude for what I had been given by others, gratitude too that I had been able to give something back. *Awakenings*, my second book, had been published the previous year.

At nearly eighty, with a scattering of medical and surgical problems, none disabling, I feel glad to be alive—"I'm glad I'm not dead!" sometimes bursts out of me when the weather is perfect. (This is in contrast to a story I heard from a friend who, walking with Samuel Beckett in Paris on a perfect spring morning, said to him, "Doesn't a day like this make you glad to be alive?" to which Beckett answered, "I wouldn't go as far as that.") I am grateful that I have experienced many things—some wonderful, some horrible—and that I have been able to write a dozen books, to receive innumerable letters from friends, colleagues, and readers, and to enjoy what Nathaniel Hawthorne called "an intercourse with the world."

I am sorry I have wasted (and still waste) so much time; I am sorry to be as agonizingly shy at eighty as I was at twenty; I am sorry that I speak no languages but my mother tongue and that I have not traveled or experienced other cultures as widely as I should have done.

I feel I should be trying to complete my life, whatever "completing a life" means. Some of my patients in their nineties or hundreds say *nunc dimittis*—"I have had a full life, and now I am ready to go." For some of them, this means going to heaven—it is always heaven rather than hell, though Samuel Johnson and James Boswell both quaked at the thought of going to hell and got furious with David Hume, who entertained no such beliefs. I have no belief in (or desire for) any postmortem existence, other than in the memories of friends and the hope that some of my books may still "speak" to people after my death.

W. H. Auden often told me he thought he would live to eighty and then "bugger off" (he lived only to sixty-seven). Though it is forty years since his death, I often dream of him, and of my parents and of former patients—all long gone but loved and important in my life.

At eighty, the specter of dementia or stroke

looms. A third of one's contemporaries are dead, and many more, with profound mental or physical damage, are trapped in a tragic and minimal existence. At eighty, the marks of decay are all too visible. One's reactions are a little slower, names more frequently elude one, and one's energies must be husbanded, but even so, one may often feel full of energy and life and not at all "old." Perhaps, with luck, I will make it, more or less intact, for another few years and be granted the liberty to continue to love and work, the two most important things, Freud insisted, in life.

When my time comes, I hope I can die in harness, as Francis Crick did. When he was told that his colon cancer had returned, at first he said nothing; he simply looked into the distance for a minute and then resumed his previous train of thought. When pressed about his diagnosis a few weeks later, he said, "Whatever has a beginning must have an end-ing." When he died, at eighty-eight, he was still fully engaged in his most creative work.

My father, who lived to ninety-four, often said that the eighties had been one of the most enjoyable decades of his life. He felt, as I begin to feel, not a shrinking but an enlargement of mental life and perspective. One has had a long experience of life, not only one's own life, but others' too. One has seen triumphs and tragedies, booms and busts, revolutions and wars, great achievements and deep ambiguities. One has seen grand theories rise, only to be toppled by stubborn facts. One is more conscious of transience and, perhaps, of beauty. At eighty, one can take a long view and have a vivid, lived sense of history not possible at an earlier age. I can imagine, feel in my bones, what a century is like, which I could not do when I was forty or sixty. I do not think of old age as an ever grimmer time that one must somehow endure and make the best of, but as a time of leisure and freedom, freed from the factitious urgencies of earlier days, free to explore whatever I wish, and to bind the thoughts and feelings of a lifetime together.

I am looking forward to being eighty.

My Own Life

A MONTH AGO, I felt that I was in good health, even robust health. At eighty-one, I still swim a mile a day. But my luck has run out—a few weeks ago I learned that I have multiple metastases in the liver. Nine years ago it was discovered that I had a rare tumor of the eye, an ocular melanoma. The radiation and lasering to remove the tumor ultimately left me blind in that eye. But though ocular melanomas metastasize in perhaps fifty percent of cases, given the particulars of my own case, the likelihood was much smaller. I am among the unlucky ones.

I feel grateful that I have been granted nine years of good health and productivity since the original diagnosis, but now I am face to face with dying. The cancer occupies a third of my liver, and though its advance may be slowed, this particular sort of cancer cannot be halted.

It is up to me now to choose how to live out the months that remain to me. I have to live in the richest, deepest, most productive way I can. In this I am encouraged by the words of one of my favorite philosophers, David Hume, who, upon learning that he was mortally ill at age sixty-five, wrote a short autobiography in a single day in April of 1776. He titled it "My Own Life."

"I now reckon upon a speedy dissolution," he wrote. "I have suffered very little pain from my disorder; and what is more strange, have, notwithstanding the great decline of my person, never suffered a moment's abatement of my spirits. . . . I possess the same ardour as ever in study, and the same gaiety in company."

I have been lucky enough to live past eighty, and the fifteen years allotted to me beyond Hume's three score and five have been equally rich in work and love. In that time, I have published five books and completed an autobiography (rather longer than Hume's few pages); I have several other books nearly finished.

Hume continued, "I am . . . a man of mild disposition, of command of temper, of an open, social, and cheerful humour, capable of attachment, but little susceptible of enmity, and of great moderation in all my passions."

Here I depart from Hume. While I have enjoyed loving relationships and friendships and have no real enmities, I cannot say (nor would anyone who knows me say) that I am a man of mild disposition. On the contrary, I am a man of vehement disposition, with violent enthusiasms, and extreme immoderation in all my passions.

And yet, one line from Hume's essay strikes

me as especially true: "It is difficult," he wrote, "to be more detached from life than I am at present."

Over the last few days, I have been able to see my life as from a great altitude, as a sort of landscape, and with a deepening sense of the connection of all its parts. This does not mean I am finished with life. On the contrary, I feel intensely alive, and I want and hope in the time that remains to deepen my friendships, to say farewell to those I love, to write more, to travel if I have the strength, to achieve new levels of understanding and insight.

This will involve audacity, clarity, and plain speaking; trying to straighten my accounts with the world. But there will be time, too, for some fun (and even some silliness, as well).

I feel a sudden clear focus and perspective. There is no time for anything inessential. I must focus on myself, my work, and my friends. I shall no longer look at the

NewsHour every night. I shall no longer pay any attention to politics or arguments about global warming.

This is not indifference but detachment—I still care deeply about the Middle East, about global warming, about growing inequality, but these are no longer my business; they belong to the future. I rejoice when I meet gifted young people—even the one who biopsied and diagnosed my metastases. I feel the future is in good hands.

I have been increasingly conscious, for the last ten years or so, of deaths among my contemporaries. My generation is on the way out, and each death I have felt as an abruption, a tearing away of part of myself. There will be no one like us when we are gone, but then there is no one like anyone else, ever. When people die, they cannot be replaced. They leave holes that cannot be filled, for it is the fate—the genetic and neural fate—of every human being to be a unique individual, to find his own path, to live his own life, to die his own death.

I cannot pretend I am without fear. But my predominant feeling is one of gratitude. I have loved and been loved; I have been given much and I have given something in return; I have read and traveled and thought and written. I have had an intercourse with the world, the special intercourse of writers and readers.

Above all, I have been a sentient being, a thinking animal, on this beautiful planet, and that in itself has been an enormous privilege and adventure.

My Periodic Table

I LOOK FORWARD EAGERLY, almost greedily, to the weekly arrival of journals like *Nature* and *Science,* and turn at once to articles on the physical sciences—not, as perhaps I should, to articles on biology and medicine. It was the physical sciences that provided my first enchantment as a boy.

In a recent issue of *Nature,* there was a thrilling article by the Nobel Prize–winning physicist Frank Wilczek on a new way of calculating the slightly different masses of neutrons and protons. The new calculation confirms that neutrons are very slightly heavier than protons, the ratio of their masses being 939.56563 to 938.27231—a trivial difference, one might think, but if it were otherwise the universe as we know it could never have developed. The ability to calculate this, Wilczek wrote, "encourages us to predict a future in which nuclear physics reaches the level of precision and versatility that atomic physics has already achieved"—a revolution that, alas, I will never see.

Francis Crick was convinced that "the hard problem"—understanding how the brain gives rise to consciousness—would be solved by 2030. "You will see it," he often said to my neuroscientist friend Ralph Siegel, "and you may too, Oliver, if you live to my age." Crick lived to his late eighties, working and thinking about consciousness till the last. Ralph died prematurely, at age fifty-two, and now I am terminally ill, at the age of eighty-two. I have to say that I am not too exercised by "the hard problem" of consciousness—indeed, I do not see it as a problem at all; but I am sad that I will not see the new nuclear physics that Wilczek envisages, nor a thousand other breakthroughs in the physical and biological sciences.

~~

A FEW WEEKS AGO, in the country, far from the lights of the city, I saw the entire sky "powdered with stars" (in Milton's words); such a sky, I imagined, could be seen only on high, dry plateaus like that of Atacama in Chile (where some of the world's most powerful telescopes are). It was this celestial splendor that suddenly made me realize how little time, how little life, I had left. My sense of the heavens' beauty, of eternity, was inseparably mixed for me with a sense of transience—and death.

I told my friends Kate and Allen, "I would like to see such a sky again when I am dying."

"We'll wheel you outside," they said.

I have been comforted, since I wrote in February about having metastatic cancer, by the hundreds of letters I have received, the expressions of love and appreciation, and the sense that (despite everything) I may have lived a good and useful life. I remain very glad and grateful for all this—yet none of it hits me as did that night sky full of stars.

I have tended since early boyhood to deal with loss—losing people dear to me—by turning to the nonhuman. When I was sent away to a boarding school as a child of six, at the outset of the Second World War, numbers became my friends; when I returned to London at ten, the elements and the periodic table became my companions. Times of stress throughout my life have led me to turn, or return, to the physical sciences, a world where there is no life, but also no death.

And now, at this juncture, when death is no longer an abstract concept, but a presence—an all-too-close, not-to-be-denied presence—I am again surrounding myself, as I did when I was a boy, with metals and minerals, little emblems of eternity. At one end of my writing table, I have element 81 in a charming box, sent to me by element-friends in England: It says, "Happy Thallium Birthday," a souvenir of my eighty-first birthday last July; then, a realm devoted to lead, element 82, for my just celebrated eighty-second birthday earlier this month. Here too is a little lead casket, containing element 90, thorium, crystalline thorium, as beautiful as diamonds, and, of course, radioactive—hence the lead casket.

━━━

AT THE START OF THE YEAR, in the weeks after I learned that I had cancer, I felt pretty well, despite my liver being half-occupied by metastases. When the cancer in my liver was treated in February by the injection of tiny beads into the hepatic arteries—a procedure called embolization—I felt awful for a couple of weeks but then super-well, charged with physical and mental energy. (The metastases had almost all been wiped out, temporarily, by the embolization.) I had been given not a remission, but an intermission, a time to deepen friendships, to see patients, to write, and to travel back to my homeland, England. People could scarcely believe at this time that I had a terminal condition, and I could easily forget it myself.

This sense of health and energy started to decline as May moved into June, but I was able to celebrate my eighty-second birthday in style. (Auden used to say that one should always celebrate one's birthday, no matter how one felt.) But now, I have some nausea and loss of appetite; chills in the day, sweats at night; and, above all, a pervasive tiredness, with sudden exhaustion if I overdo things. I continue to swim daily, but more slowly now, as I am beginning to feel a little short of breath. I could deny it before, but I know I am ill now. A CT scan on July 7 confirmed that the metastases had not only regrown in my liver but had now spread beyond it as well.

I started a new sort of treatment—immunotherapy—last week. It is not without its hazards, but I hope it will give me a few more good months. But before beginning this, I wanted to have a little fun: a trip to North Carolina to see the wonderful lemur research center at Duke University. Lemurs are close to the ancestral stock from which all primates arose, and I am happy to think that one of my own ancestors, fifty million years ago, was a little tree-dwelling creature not so dissimilar to the lemurs of today. I love their leaping vitality, their inquisitive nature.

NEXT TO THE CIRCLE of lead on my table is the land of bismuth: naturally occurring bismuth from Australia; little limousine-shaped ingots of bismuth from a mine in

Bolivia; bismuth slowly cooled from a melt to form beautiful iridescent crystals terraced like a Hopi village; and, in a nod to Euclid and the beauty of geometry, a cylinder and a sphere made of bismuth.

Bismuth is element 83. I do not think I will see my eighty-third birthday, but I feel there is something hopeful, something encouraging, about having "83" around. Moreover, I have a soft spot for bismuth, a modest grey metal, often unregarded, ignored, even by metal lovers. My feeling as a doctor for the mistreated or marginalized extends into the inorganic world and finds a parallel in my feeling for bismuth.

I almost certainly will not see my polonium (eighty-fourth) birthday, nor would I want any polonium around, with its intense, murderous radioactivity. But then, at the other end of my table—my periodic table—I have a beautifully machined piece of beryllium (element 4) to remind me of my childhood, and of how long ago my soon-to-end life began.

Sabbath

MY MOTHER and her seventeen brothers and sisters had an Orthodox
upbringing—all photographs of their father
show him wearing a yarmulke, and I was told
that he woke up if it fell off during the night.
My father too came from an Orthodox back-
ground. Both my parents were very conscious
of the Fourth Commandment ("Remember
the Sabbath day, to keep it holy"), and the Sabbath (Shabbos, as we called it in our Litvak
way) was entirely different from the rest of the
week. No work was allowed, no driving, no use
of the telephone; it was forbidden to switch on
a light or a stove. Being physicians, my parents made exceptions. They could not take the
phone off the hook or completely avoid driv-

ing; they had to be available, if necessary, to see patients, or operate, or deliver babies.

We lived in a fairly Orthodox Jewish community in Cricklewood, in Northwest London—the butcher, the baker, the grocer, the greengrocer, the fishmonger, all closed their shops in good time for the Sabbath, and did not open their shutters till Sunday morning. All of them, and all our neighbors, we imagined, were celebrating Shabbos in much the same fashion as we did.

Around midday on Friday, my mother doffed her surgical identity and attire and devoted herself to making gefilte fish and other delicacies for Shabbos. Just before evening fell, she would light the ritual candles, cupping their flames with her hands, and murmuring a prayer. We would all put on clean, fresh Shabbos clothes, and gather for the first meal of the Sabbath, the evening meal. My father would lift his silver wine cup and chant the blessings and the Kiddush, and after the meal, he would lead us all in chanting the grace.

On Saturday mornings, my three brothers and I trailed our parents to Cricklewood Synagogue on Walm Lane, a huge shul built in the 1930s to accommodate part of the exodus of Jews from the East End to Cricklewood at that time. The shul was always full during my boyhood, and we all had our assigned seats, the men downstairs, the women—my mother, various aunts and cousins—upstairs; as a little boy, I sometimes waved to them during the service. Though I could not understand the Hebrew in the prayer book, I loved its sound and especially hearing the old medieval prayers sung, led by our wonderfully musical hazan.

All of us met and mingled outside the synagogue after the service—and we would usually walk to the house of my Auntie Florrie and her three children to say a Kiddush, accompanied by sweet red wine and honey cakes, just enough to stimulate our appetites for lunch. After a cold lunch at home—gefilte fish, poached salmon, beetroot jelly—Saturday afternoons, if not interrupted by emergency medical calls for my parents, would be devoted to family visits. Uncles and aunts and cousins would visit us for tea, or we them; we all lived within walking distance of one another.

THE SECOND WORLD WAR decimated our Jewish community in Cricklewood, and the Jewish community in England as a whole was to lose thousands of people in the post-war years. Many Jews, including cousins of mine, emigrated to Israel; others went to Australia, Canada, or the States; my eldest brother, Marcus, went to Australia in 1950. Many of those who stayed assimilated and adopted diluted, attenuated forms of Judaism. Our synagogue, which would be packed to capacity when I was a child, grew emptier by the year.

I chanted my bar mitzvah portion in 1946 to a relatively full synagogue, including several dozen of my relatives, but this, for me, was the end of formal Jewish practice. I did not embrace the ritual duties of a Jewish adult—praying every day, putting on tefillin before prayer each weekday morning—and I gradually became more indifferent to the beliefs and habits of my parents, though there was no particular point of rupture until I was eighteen. It was then that my father, enquiring into my sexual feelings, compelled me to admit that I liked boys.

"I haven't done anything," I said, "it's just a feeling—but don't tell Ma, she won't be able to take it."

He did tell her, and the next morning she came down with a look of horror on her face, and shrieked at me: "You are an abomination.

I wish you had never been born." (She was no doubt thinking of the verse in Leviticus that read, "If a man also lie with mankind, as he lieth with a woman, both of them have committed an abomination: They shall surely be put to death; their blood shall be upon them.")

The matter was never mentioned again, but her harsh words made me hate religion's capacity for bigotry and cruelty.

After I qualified as a doctor in 1960, I removed myself abruptly from England and what family and community I had there, and went to the New World, where I knew nobody. When I moved to Los Angeles, I found a sort of community among the weight lifters on Muscle Beach, and with my fellow neurology residents at U.C.L.A., but I craved some deeper connection—"meaning"—in my life, and it was the absence of this, I think, that drew me into near-suicidal addiction to amphetamines in the 1960s.

Recovery started, slowly, as I found meaningful work in New York, in a chronic care hospital in the Bronx (the "Mount Carmel" I wrote about in *Awakenings*). I was fascinated by my patients there, cared for them deeply, and felt something of a mission to tell their stories—stories of situations virtually unknown, almost unimaginable, to the general public and, indeed, to many of my colleagues. I had discovered my vocation, and this I pursued doggedly, single-mindedly, with little encouragement from my colleagues. Almost unconsciously, I became a storyteller at a time when medical narrative was almost extinct. This did not dissuade me, for I felt my roots lay in the great neurological case histories of the nineteenth century (and I was encouraged here by the great Russian neuro-psychologist A. R. Luria). It was a lonely but deeply satisfying, almost monkish existence that I was to lead for many years.

DURING THE 1990S, I came to know a cousin and contemporary of mine, Robert John Aumann, a man of remarkable appearance with his robust, athletic build and long white beard that made him, even at sixty, look like an ancient sage. He is a man of great intellectual power but also of great human warmth and tenderness, and deep religious commitment—indeed, "commitment" is one of his favorite words. Although, in his work, he stands for rationality in economics and human affairs, there is no conflict for him between reason and faith.

He insisted I have a mezuzah on my door, and brought me one from Israel. "I know you don't believe," he said, "but you should have one anyhow." I didn't argue.

In a remarkable 2004 interview, Robert John spoke of his lifelong work in mathematics and game theory, but also of his family—how he would go skiing and mountaineering with some of his nearly thirty children and grandchildren (a kosher cook, carrying saucepans, would accompany them), and the importance of the Sabbath to him.

"The observance of the Sabbath is extremely beautiful," he said, "and is impossible without being religious. It is not even a question of improving society—it is about improving one's own quality of life."

In December of 2005, Robert John received a Nobel Prize for his fifty years of fundamental work in economics. He was not entirely an easy guest for the Nobel Committee, for he went to Stockholm with his family, including many of those children and grandchildren, and all had to have special kosher plates, utensils, and food, and special formal clothes, with no biblically forbidden admixture of wool and linen.

That same month, I was found to have cancer in one eye, and while I was in the hospital for treatment the following month, Robert John visited. He was full of entertaining stories about the Nobel Prize and the ceremony in Stockholm, but made a point of saying that, had he been compelled to travel to Stockholm on a Saturday, he would have refused the prize. His commitment to the Sabbath, its utter peacefulness and remoteness from worldly concerns, would have trumped even a Nobel.

IN 1955, as a twenty-two-year-old, I went to Israel for several months to work on a kibbutz, and though I enjoyed it, I decided not to go again. Even though so many of my cousins had moved there, the politics of the Middle East disturbed me, and I suspected I would be out of place in a deeply religious society. But in the spring of 2014, hearing that my cousin Marjorie—a physician who had been a protégée of my mother's and had worked in the field of medicine till the age of ninety-eight—was nearing death, I phoned her in Jerusalem to say farewell. Her voice was unexpectedly strong and resonant, with an accent very much like my mother's. "I don't intend to die now," she said; "I will be having my hundredth birthday on June eighteenth. Will you come?"

I said, "Yes, of course!" When I hung up, I realized that I had, within a few seconds, reversed a decision of almost sixty years.

It was purely a family visit. I celebrated Marjorie's hundredth birthday with her and extended family. I saw two other cousins dear to me in my London days, innumerable second and removed cousins, and, of course, Robert John. I felt embraced by my family in a way I had not known since childhood.

I had felt a little fearful visiting my Ortho-dox family with my lover, Billy—my mother's words still echoed in my mind—but Billy too was warmly received. How profoundly attitudes had changed, even among the Orthodox, was made clear by Robert John when he invited Billy and me to join him and his family at their opening Sabbath meal.

The peace of the Sabbath, of a stopped world, a time outside time, was palpable, infused everything, and I found myself drenched with a wistfulness, something akin to nostalgia, wondering what if: What if A and B and C had been different? What sort of person might I have been? What sort of a life might I have lived?

In December 2014, I completed my memoir *On the Move* and gave the manuscript to my publisher, not dreaming that days later I would learn I had metastatic cancer, coming from the melanoma I had in my eye nine years earlier. I am glad I was able to complete my memoir without knowing this, and that I had been able, for the first time in my life, to make a full and frank declaration of my sexuality, facing the world openly, with no more guilty secrets locked up inside me.

In February, I felt I had to be equally open about my cancer—and facing death. I was, in fact, in the hospital when my essay on this, "My Own Life," was published in *The New York Times.* In July I wrote another piece for the paper, "My Periodic Table," in which the physical cosmos, and the elements I loved, took on lives of their own.

And now, weak, short of breath, my once-firm muscles melted away by cancer, I find my thoughts, increasingly, not on the supernatural or spiritual but on what is meant by living a good and worthwhile life—achieving a sense of peace within oneself. I find my thoughts drifting to the Sabbath, the day of rest, the seventh day of the week, and perhaps the seventh day of one's life as well, when one can feel that one's work is done, and one may, in good conscience, rest.

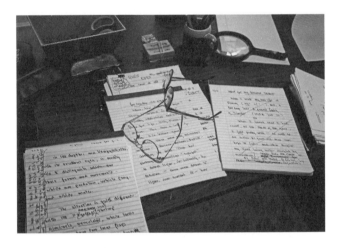

Oliver Sacks was born in 1933 in London and was educated at Queen's College, Oxford. He completed his medical training at San Francisco's Mount Zion Hospital and at UCLA before moving to New York, where he soon encountered the patients whom he would write about in his book *Awakenings.*

Dr. Sacks spent almost fifty years working as a neurologist and wrote many books, including *The Man Who Mistook His Wife for a Hat*, *Musicophilia*, and *Hallucinations*, about the strange neurological predicaments and conditions of his patients. *The New York Times* referred to him as "the poet laureate of medicine," and over the years he received many awards, including honors from the Guggenheim Foundation, the National Science Foundation, the American Academy of Arts and Letters, and the Royal College of Physicians. His memoir, *On the Move*, was published shortly before his death in August 2015.

For more information, please visit www.oliversacks.com.

ALL PHOTOGRAPHS BY BILL HAYES

www.billhayes.com

A NOTE ON THE TYPE

The text of this book was composed in Trump Mediaeval. It was designed by Professor Georg Trump (1896–1985) in the mid-1950s. The roman letterforms are based on classical prototypes, but Professor Trump has imbued them with his own unmistakable style. The italic letterforms, unlike those of so many other typefaces, are closely related to their roman counterparts. The result is a truly contemporary type, notable for both its legibility and its versatility.

Composed by North Market Street Graphics, Lancaster, Pennsylvania

Printed and bound by Thomson-Shore, Dexter, Michigan

Designed by Iris Weinstein